My *Life*

Tina Atkins

ISBN 978-1-63814-693-3 (Paperback)
ISBN 978-1-63814-694-0 (Digital)

The events and details depicted in the book are true. The names have been changed in order to protect the people involved.

Covenant Books, Inc.
11661 Hwy 707
Murrells Inlet, SC 29576
www.covenantbooks.com

This book is dedicated to my loving Father God, who has seen me through every trial and hardship in life! *I love you!*

Contents

Chapter 1

The Beginning of Life

Caroline—my world, my everything, my momma! She was born February 27, 1963, to my grandmom who had eleven children. Due to circumstances, they weren't all raised together. Some of them wound up in foster care, and some she was able to keep. I don't really know the details of who kept my mom or if she ended up in foster care. But despite all of that, she was my rock, my love, my everything.

What a beautiful woman, tall with a thin frame. She always had a smile on her face and could make you laugh no matter how you felt. Talk about brightening up a room when you walk in! She was the epitome of that, one of the sweetest people I had the privilege of knowing. In her own way, she was family oriented and loved her kids. Even though she was mentally challenged and didn't grasp things as quickly as other people, she made an effort to be with us.

Our tradition was sitting and eating candy, whether it was on the corner store steps or eating it in the house. She always found the time to spend with us even if it was just sitting and not saying anything or making sure we didn't need anything. Even though she didn't get to do many things because she was sick most of my younger life, when she was well, my brother, sister, and I would sit and enjoy her company. Those were the times that helped me get through the hard trials in my life.

I was born December 4, 1987, in Camden, New Jersey. I remember Camden like the back of my hand. It was a city where crime was expected and tolerated. No one wanted to visit or even go because of all the drug dealers, prostitutes, and pimps who ran the streets. We were known as one of the most dangerous cities in the world at one point. Sewage, trash, and cigarettes lined the sides of the streets. Every other house was abandoned or torn down. There were countless prostitutes and drug dealers that did their business in the abandoned houses or just on the street because no one dared to stop them. The look of some of the drug dealers was "I dare someone to say something to me." The prostitutes looked scared, lonely, and wished someone would rescue them. Some of the girls were as young as fifteen or sixteen. Sometimes I thought this will always be a haven for the bad.

It seemed like nobody cared about our city, not even the police. It's sad to say, but it felt like a huge cloud of depression, sadness, and hopelessness drove the city. Despite all of that, Camden also had the people that made it feel like a community. Some of the grandmas, granddads, and adults would sit on their porches sewing, barbecuing, hanging up clothes, or just watching as people went by. We had good people who would look out for the teenagers, kids, and even some of the adults that got caught in the life (drugs and prostitution) or were trying to get out. Some of them would say, "There's more to this life than prostitution or selling drugs. You have a future ahead of you. This is not the end." Some of them would look and smile. Although I don't know, but I believe those grandmas, granddads, and adults made a difference in their lives.

I can't forget about the people that ran the dance companies to keep girls off the streets or the men that ran the sports facilities or after-school programs to give guys a chance to grow into men and not go into the drug life. We also had the after-school programs that took kids in until the parents got off work. Some of the parents worked two and three jobs to support their kids. Camden was like a blessing and a curse at the same time. It opened my eyes to the harsh realities of the world but also taught me there's good people no matter where you are. This was my home though, and I am grateful that I got to see so many different lifestyles because this environment helped me become the woman I am today.

My home life mirrored that of Camden's environment, from the evil to the hateful attitude of some of the drug dealers. From what I was told, I was a small baby who liked to laugh. The same goes for my sister and brothers. Elizabeth was born December 4, 1986. Elizabeth was more like a mom to me. She's a year older than me. She looked out for my brothers and me and tried to make sure we were happy and knew how to do basic things. She taught me how to whistle, how to blow bubble gum, and what to do when my period started. No matter what, Elizabeth always looked worried and like she had a lot on her mind.

I don't think she was happy. I was always worried about her because she didn't seem like she was here, even though her body was, which is understandable because I wasn't happy either. I wish I could take her sadness away.

Elizabeth was my rock through the hard times. *I love her so much*! She never had the chance to be a child, none of us did, but more so for her because she took care of our brothers and me. She was strong for my mom, brothers, and I. Elizabeth reminded me of a small adult. I remember she was about seven or eight, and she was in charge of giving my youngest brother his shots because he was born with AIDS. She was and continues to be one of the strongest women I know. I am and will always be proud of her for stepping up because it wasn't easy at all. I know you had the weight of the world on you, sister, but I thank you from the bottom of my heart.

My brothers were born October 17, 1985, and 1991. My oldest brother, Derrick, is intellectually challenged. He always had a small frame no matter what he ate, and he could eat. This made me jealous because he never gained weight. He's always happy and full of light. This was a help because he didn't understand the abuse that was going on which was good. He was always smiling and asking us if we're okay. He loved to play with cars and building blocks and other boy toys. He had a huge collection of cars that he played with for hours. I loved watching him in his element. He is a piece of my heart.

My last brother, Daniel, was born with AIDS which meant he was always sick. But that didn't stop him from smiling. He was a beautiful tan color, so small and fragile.

His spirit and soul were so strong. He always lit up the room when he came in because he would be smiling from ear to ear no matter how much pain he was in. He was like our mom in that way. Everybody loved him, from his nurses to his aides to his friends. He was the sweetest little boy. I believe God brought him into this world to help all who encounter him become better people. I love you, Daniel.

I never met my dad. I couldn't tell you if he was White, Black, or anything. Honestly, I don't know if he knows I exist. I believe he was one of the men my mom met while she was a prostitute. Although I don't really think about it, a part of me goes through pain and wishes he knew I existed. I felt like maybe if he knew, he could have saved us, helped us, or even just loved us. I knew that would not happen because my mom never even mentioned him. I don't think she knew who he was because of the type of work she did.

We lived in this awful little hotel room that consisted of two beds. The room smelled awful. We lived with rats, bugs, and every little creepy crawler you can think of. I didn't know it at the time, but we lived like this because my momma was a prostitute. It was home to us though, and we didn't know any better, so we made the best of it. I remember us jumping from bed to bed in the apartment to avoid getting bit by rats. We ate, played games, and just had fun. This was our home, and we made the best of it because this was all we knew.

One time we were jumping from bed to bed playing, and I fell and broke my ankle. My mom picked me up and carried me all the way to the hospital with my brother and sister following close behind. It was pitch-black outside, so we used the streetlights to see. The hospital was about six blocks away from the hotel. They put a cast on me, and my mom carried me back to the hotel. When we got back home, I tried to play with my brother and sister but couldn't move much due to my leg. My mom left again to go to work, so we just watched TV and played card games with each other.

I don't really remember my mom's voice or her talking much, probably because it's been so many years since I heard it, but what I do remember is that she was very sweet, and she always made us feel loved the best she could despite everything she was going through. I always talked to her about what I was going through and what I was feeling. I don't remember her responding, but I do remember her smiling at me as I shared.

My mom started going to this church as she got older. We went with two of my aunts. All three of them were looking to get closer to God and just find purpose in life. The church seemed okay in my little mind and like they really loved the Lord. As my mom kept going, she started getting closer to God and trying to make herself a better person. She would make an effort to prepare our lunch. She was happy and able to function. It seemed like she was moving in a better place in her mind, heart, and life as best she could.

My mother was a prostitute and practically lived on the street. She would leave us alone in the hotel to go work, and my sister Elizabeth would take care of us. She worked all the time and would come home sad, depressed, and smelly. She had bruises on her face and body. She was very skinny and barely ate. I remember hearing her cry in the shower but step out of it like nothing was wrong. No matter what, in my little head I would always think, *I love you, Mama. No matter how sad you are, to me you are still the greatest person.*

I had hope though because as soon as she attended this church, everything seemed to change for the better. She was happy, we were happy, and everything seemed to be getting better. She even stopped stripping and prostituting to focus on us. Then out of nowhere, my momma started going back to prostitution again, and slowly but surely, our life started going back to how it was before. After this happened, everything changed. A little time later, she found out she was pregnant with my little brother, Daniel. She went to the hospital and discovered she had AIDS. My mom was so weak from prostituting and contracting AIDS. It was really hard seeing her like that. She had no strength at all. So my little brother was born with AIDS. DCF (Department of Children and Families) was threatening to take us again if she didn't get help. She got help the best way she could from the church. My aunts wanted us to come live with them so we could be together. I was around three at the time. My mom unfortunately was listening to what the church people said to her. I don't blame her though because she was in the church, and you would expect them to do the right thing. Unfortunately, we learned quickly what they were really about.

Chapter 2

Everything Has Changed

My mom met this lady from the church who seemed nice and innocent. She convinced her to come live with her because DCF had already tried taking us before when she became a prostitute. Now they were about to take us again, so she convinced my mom that it would be better for all five of us to come live with her. What started out as good quickly turned evil!

We were three, four, and five when we went to go live with Greta. Greta was a single lady who had three children of her own—Ronald who was the oldest; Nicholas, the second; and Victoria, the last. They were about five years and older than us. Greta reminded me of a scary witch (no lie), but in my mind, I was thinking she can't be all that bad because she took five of us in at the same time, all the while she had three children of her own.

Greta was deep in church. All the adults around her were deep in church. It was a medium-sized church with an apostle and pastor who led the church with a passion about them that was beautiful. We were in church every single day for about ten hours at the least. Sundays, we started with 4:00 a.m. prayer for about two hours, then we had church for about five hours. After that, there was an afterglow which means they go in the back and talk about the service and what they got out of it. When they were finished, they would come out to the lobby and have another session of talking. While they were doing this, us children and teenagers would be in the church talking, laughing, playing Uno, or doing schoolwork. Then we would be on our way to the car, and they would stop and talk again. Finally, after all those hours, we get to go home around five or six o'clock. We were exhausted by then.

On Mondays, the church had what they called the table where Greta and other members brought food for them to eat and talk about the service and what they feel God is doing in their lives and what they are going through. I always thought, *This is so boring, and how much stuff can y'all talk about.* I thought this because they talked about the same stuff every week, and nothing changed. They still had the same problems and issues but would converse every week to talk a bunch of empty nothings! I never understood because I remember the apostle preaching God can do anything, and he can change everything that you're going through if you have faith and believe. So hey, I thought they were just faking it and not really believing what the apostle was preaching.

On Tuesdays, they had prayer or a get-together and talked again. On Wednesdays, they had service, praise and worship, and then a preaching from the apostle. On Thursdays, we had prayer, then they talked for a little, then we went home. Fridays, we had service again, praise and worship, then preaching again. On Saturdays, they had men and women fellowship. The women talked among themselves about what was going on in their lives or about their children and husbands. The men did the same thing in their group.

One particular time, we were having women's fellowship, and one of the ladies was sharing that her daughter was talking back and not listening. The pastor said, "If you don't stop, God is gonna get you."

The young lady started crying and saying, "No, I don't want God to get me because he's really gonna get me, and I will be in trouble."

The pastor responded, "Oh, wow, you really believe God is gonna get you. Wow, I didn't even think that."

This made me think, *If y'all don't believe God will convict us, then why are you trying to make us believe it?* I was confused.

This was the kind of church where you could not wear pants. You had to follow every single thing they said, and they tried to make sure that every person that came in there would follow their way of thinking and believing by taking the scriptures out of context. We couldn't listen to any other music because it was considered of the devil, and if you listened to him, you were his daughter or son.

We always fasted for I don't know what. I guess to get closer to God and kill our own desires. As the years went by, the church fluctuated between lots of members and then a few. Everyone took the apostle's word as law. They did not make a move with their lives without his say-so. For example, one of the ladies wanted to visit her sister, and she would not go for years until the apostle said it's okay. When people would visit the church, some people would fall in line, and others would call us an occult because of the strict rules and control. I always thought they were crazy and of the devil. You don't know what you're talking about if you don't go here. In the back of my head, I felt there was a shred of truth to what they were talking about, but I didn't want to acknowledge it because I was going here, and I still believed we were doing the right thing by following the apostle and what God says.

In my earlier years, my sister and I went to a public school from kindergarten to fourth grade. It was amazing. We got to associate with people other than the church members. We met so many different types of teachers and students. I loved it and wished we could stay there. We played games like parachute and dodgeball. I loved to learn, so my head was always in a book and trying to learn new things.

I had a favorite teacher, Mr. Belmont. He was so alert and always asked how each one of us was doing every single day. I was going through so much in my short life. I don't know If he could tell something was not right, but he was always so sweet. Whenever he saw me, he would ask, "Are you okay?"' or "How is your home life?" I knew he saw something wasn't right when he saw my face, but I always lied and said everything was okay because I thought I was strong enough to handle it, and I was scared of the consequences of sharing about the abuse. I was too ashamed to tell anybody what was going on. Mr. Belmont never stopped asking though for as long as I went there. I appreciate him, and he will always hold a place in my heart.

When I got in the fifth grade, Elizabeth, Victoria, Ronald, Nicholas, and I started attending the church school. The school was good at first. In the early days, the church and school were located in a motel that was used as a strip club before the apostle had it torn down and turned into the church and school. The school was hot on hot days, and it seemed we would freeze to death in the wintertime. Our teachers were attentive at first, then some of them started not coming to class. We wore uniforms, which was easy; we didn't need to pick out clothes. We wore these black and white shoes that were awful, with white stockings. We had white shirts with red blazers or sweaters on top. Our skirts and dresses were red, white, and black. The uniforms were okay, but those shoes were awful. We wore this every day until we finally graduated from the twelfth grade. We attended school at this building until I was in the seventh grade.

At the end of my seventh grade, we moved to a building the church bought. It's a building with lots of rooms for different things. The building is pinkish with a grayish roof. We had different classes like science, history, math, spelling, praise and worship, and Bible. Some of our teachers taught multiple subjects. For example, our history teacher taught art and dance. Our gym teacher taught praise, worship, and gym. If our teachers did not show up, we just talked and played in the room. I was a very quiet, miserable, and shy kid. I was going through so much abuse. I was teased because I had big breasts, and I slouched when I sat down.

I pretended it didn't bother me, but I died a little every time it happened. I loved school despite the teasing because it was an escape from home life and, I loved to learn. I was picked on throughout my schooling, but it wasn't that bad to the point where I wanted to drop out. I just endured it because it was still better than being at the house. I didn't say anything because I was quite good at masking my pain and hurt, plus I knew no one could do anything about it, so I just left it alone. We had about thirty people in the whole school. The school went from kindergarten to twelfth grade. It was really small. Our teachers were members of the church. Our teachers, when they were there, did their best to make sure we learned and understood the material.

I really loved my Bible teacher. He was a nice man who was extremely passionate about the Bible and God. He was one of the first people who actually got me interested in the Bible and wanting to learn more about God. I admired him and his lifestyle so much. He loved his family and the church with his whole heart. I also really loved my math teacher, Mrs. Betty. Mrs. Betty always encouraged me and told me I could do better, and in return, it motivated me to get As and try my best. She made sure we knew the material. Mrs. Betty was also one of my favorite people outside of school. She is so nice and understanding. I always loved her relationship with her husband, Mr. Jacob. They really loved each other and just were kind people. They were and still are an example to me of a happily married couple. Despite everything, they are still together and still holding each other up. School was overall a good place.

Derrick went to a different school because he was intellectually challenged. He really liked it because they taught stuff on his level, and he understood and got it. He wound up graduating with his high school diploma. I'm so proud of him. In our school life, we saw the same people every day from church to school.

Our home life was—I don't even know how to describe it, so I will start with describing the foster family. How to describe the foster family? I described Greta a little bit earlier, but let me go in more detail. She reminded me of a mean witch who pretended to play nice. Greta was very nice when we first met, and she tried to be accommodating as much as her character would let her be. She was a round woman who wore her glasses on her nose and always looked constipated. She was controlling and wanted things done her way no matter what. Greta was a foster parent and had lots of kids stay with her throughout the years. As we got older, Greta got more evil. She would beat us for stupid stuff and make us sit outside of her room for hours if we stole something because we were hungry or if we were trying to find something to wear to church. One time, she took turns beating us until we had welts, bruises, and marks all over our bodies because one of us took food because we were hungry. Even when she saw the marks, she didn't stop. She just kept on beating us, took a break when she got tired, then resumed. She only stopped because she realized none of us would say anything. Every Saturday, Friday, and Wednesday, we would stand outside her room for hours showing her clothes, until she approved an outfit we could wear to church. She would fall asleep while we were showing her. If we stopped and went to bed, she would find us, slap us, and say, "Did I say you could go to bed?" So we would continually wake her up to show her clothes until she says we can go to bed. She kept getting bigger and bigger as she got older.

Ronald, her oldest son, was in the army, so he was gone for spurts at a time, but he seemed nice but weird. Ronald was of regular build and always looked serious but had stuff on his mind. He wore glasses sometimes. He kind of had a smirk and a sneaky face when he smiled. To me, he looked like he always had a hidden agenda. He was Greta's favorite child, and he could do no wrong in her eyes.

Nicholas was strong-willed and told it like it is (he was my favorite). He is of medium build with a dark complexion. He was and still is one of the funniest people I've ever met. He has such a good heart. He's strong-willed and doesn't care what anybody thinks. He was chocolate and reminded me of a king by the way he would act. Greta and he would go head-to-head because of the way she treated us. He would fuss and ask her why we were being abused like that or what did we do to deserve this punishment. Her response always was "they deserve it because they're bad" or we didn't follow what the Bible said about us obeying her. He would get us out the punishment 10 percent of the time which I appreciated. The other 90 percent, we were still punished. I love Nicholas because no matter what, even if he didn't get us out of it, he still made an effort to defend us. He didn't get special treatment at all, and he got yelled at and told off just like us because he defended us and was strong-willed, but that never deterred him.

Victoria was a spoiled child who was just like her mama. She was of average build also, and she just had a spoiled evil vibe about her. She and her mom were cut from the same cloth. Even how her and her mom looked at us, you could see the devil in their eyes and characters. She made our lives hell, along with her mom. Whatever she wanted, she got. There was no type of *no* in her vocabulary, no matter what she asked for. Victoria was ridiculously spoiled! If somebody did eventually say no to her, she would get upset and stomp and cry like a baby. Now remember she was like five years older than us, so imagine that sight, embarrassing.

Even though Greta was evil, she had great taste in decorating. The house was impeccable. The outside of the house had a beautiful yard where flowers grew in the front of it. It looked like a usual suburban home. The outside was painted white and had a red roof. It was really nice. Our neighbors were about fifty feet from us. We had a gate in the backyard. We lived in a beautiful house with four bedrooms, so all the girls slept in one room. There were two bedrooms at the top and two on the bottom.

Elizabeth and I had bunk beds. Victoria had her own bed on the left side of the wall. We were on the right side of the wall. Our room had a bench that sat right in front of the window. It was super cool. Sometimes we would play with our Barbies and look out the window at the world. We kept our teddy bears and Barbie dolls on the table. It was so colorful. We had a huge closet with all our clothes in it. The closet went far back, so we were able to keep our sweaters and other items in there. We used to steal Ensure milk along with other items. We had bags of Ensure cans hidden back there. That closet was a great hiding place. We got discovered and got whopped, but it was worth it. They were good, and we were hungry. We had a pretty pink light in the corner. It was a nice room.

Ronald and Nicholas had their own room at first, until we came along; same with Victoria. Once we came, Derrick, Nicholas, and Ronald shared a room. Their room was located downstairs. They had bunk beds like us which Nicholas and Derrick shared. Ronald had his own bed. The bunk beds were on the right, and the twin bed was on the left. Their room was gray, white, and blue. They had nice pictures of cars, spiritual sayings, and paintings on the wall. The room had a cool slanted window in there. You could actually sit in the window because it was slanted upward. It was really cool. The room was small, and you could barely walk in it, but it accommodated them and their stuff. The hallway had extra closets for the items that didn't fit in the room.

My youngest brother, Daniel, contracted AIDS from my mom when he was born, so when he was younger, he rarely stayed in the house. He always stayed at this facility that treats and takes care of young kids aged twelve and younger. When he stayed on the weekends, he would stay in my mom's room, and the nurses would take care of both of them. My mom had gotten so weak that she could barely get out of bed. Eventually, she was confined to the bed and had to get assistance for everything she needed to do. She had her own room upstairs. It was painted three different colors of blue. The ceiling was dark blue, the walls were sky blue, and the floor was ocean blue. The color combination was weird. She had a small closet and a huge shelf in her room that kept her medicines, sheets, vials, clothes, and any other things the doctor and nurses needed to take care of her. I didn't like going in there because it felt cold and uninviting. It's like the heart and soul left the room. I went in there anyway to look at my mom and talk to her. The only thing that was in the room was my mom's hospital bed and her shelf with all her medicines and stuff she needed. She constantly had nurses and doctors in her room to change, feed, and clothe her. In 1995, I don't think they knew a whole lot about the medicines and treatments for AIDS or how to help my mom live with it and keep it under control. I think that's why she went so quickly. She lived for about four years after we knew she had it, but now I see people who lived with AIDS for many years. She didn't really have love in the room, just people doing their job. I always wondered how my mom felt as she sat in the room alone some nights.

Greta's room was downstairs. Her room colors were white and burgundy. It was really pretty. The walls were painted white, and she had burgundy curtains over her windows. She also had lots of pictures of red and white flowers on the walls. The room had a burgundy bedspread with white sheets. The furniture was burgundy and white. She had a bathroom in her room which was white with a big tub and shower. The bathroom was decorated the same with white walls and a burgundy toothbrush holder and soap holders. The bathroom had a burgundy shower curtain with white and light-burgundy flowers and burgundy floor mats.

There were three bathrooms in the house, one upstairs for us girls and my mom, the other one downstairs for the boys. The last one was in Greta's room. The house had a living room and dining room mainly decorated white, black, and burgundy, which were Greta's favorite colors. It was really pretty. The dining room had a huge table in the middle of it with fake white and burgundy flowers on it. The chairs were burgundy with white and burgundy pillows on top of them. We had brownish tile on the floor. The living room had a huge burgundy sectional and love seat in it. It had beautiful gray soft carpet throughout the living room. I loved to sit or lay on the carpet and think about life. The walls were white with picture frames of flowers, pictures, inspirational and other quotes hanging on them, along with other beautiful art pieces. The living room was big, so it was able to accommodate a fifty-inch TV on a black TV stand. Behind the TV was a long and huge ledge that expanded the whole area of the living room. We would sometimes play on it because it was able to hold our weight. I thought it was really cool because I never saw, and still never had seen, one like this in a house except ours.

The kitchen was medium sized and filled with burgundy and white utensils, pots, and pans. It was very sleek and clean, decorated in what colors? You guessed it—burgundy, black, and white. The kitchen had lots of sayings on big forks and spoons hanging on the wall. I can't remember even one of them though. The house also had a basement where we stored a lot of extra items we had, like washing powder, winter clothes, furniture, and other items we weren't using. The washer and dryer were located in the basement also. The basement was nice and clean with gray-and-white walls and brown floorboards. I didn't like going down there because it was scary, dark, and I heard weird noises. The basement was decorated gray. We had a small attic too which wasn't decorated. It just had extra items in it. It was brown and plain. We stayed on this quiet street where all the homes were beautiful. We lived here for about four years before we got evicted. We came home from a conference with an eviction notice on the door. I don't remember where we went, but we stayed somewhere until we got another house. Unfortunately, we moved so much because Greta couldn't afford to pay the bills. My foundation was more unstable because we moved so much. I became even more weird and withdrawn due to the uncertainty of where I was going to lay my head every night. All the homes we moved to were beautiful. We just couldn't afford any of them. Too bad family life wasn't beautiful like the houses we lived in.

Chapter 3

Dark Nights

The sexual, physical, emotional, and mind abuse began about a month after we moved in. It was like they just couldn't wait any more to torture us. The first time it happened, I was four years old. I was sleeping in my bed when all of a sudden, I felt somebody on top of me. I thought I was dreaming but opened my eyes to find Ronald on top of me. I remember thinking in my little head, *This has got to be a dream. Is this normal? What is happening? Mommy! What is he doing? This doesn't feel natural. I'm terrified! I'm scared!* He didn't actually put his penis inside of me, just on top of my bare vagina and bare chest. He moved up and down. When he was finished, he would ejaculate on my stomach, which I didn't know that's what it was until I was older. When he was finished, he just got up and wiped the semen off my stomach with a towel. He never said anything. I just lay there in horror and disbelief. That was the beginning of the abuse.

When he was abusing me, most of the time, I would pretend to be asleep. I don't know why. I think it helped me get through it also or helped me not face him because I was scared. I think he knew I wasn't asleep. I don't think he cared though. When I wasn't being abused by him, I was being abused by the foster lady, physically and emotionally. She called us dumb, stupid, retarded, saying we will never amount to anything. Every time she would say these words, I would look at her, and my face would be stone-cold. Alone, I would cry and feel like it's true. I will never amount to anything; she's right. She punished us for any and everything. If we spoke too loud or laughed (I'm not joking), we were punished. We were not allowed to say I'm sick because it wasn't of God, meaning if we were sick, we just had to pray about it or say I'm healed, even though we weren't. So we would just be sick and try and find our own remedies like noodles or hot showers, then lay in the bed.

She found any excuse to make our lives miserable. We were not allowed to go anywhere, and we got beaten mercilessly. We got beaten with anything she could find—hangers, belts, the piece that goes to the blinds (oh god, I hated that thing), extension cords. We always had welts and huge black-and-blue bruises all over our bodies from the neck down. I remember not being able to sit for days at a time or trying to sit at school but barely able to.

One time, we got in trouble for something she made up. We were cleaning and doing everything she said that day. The church was having a huge Christmas party, and my sister and I couldn't go because of something she made up. I tell you we cried so hard that night. We didn't say words to each other; we just cried. I believe we cried so hard because she was getting away with the abuse. We knew we didn't do anything, and she was doing anything she wanted to us and getting away with it. We cried ourselves to sleep that night. It was the type of pain and hurt where no words could form, but you had to just let it out through tears. I really couldn't tell anybody how she was treating us because they were on her side with even the little things she would do in front of them. She would always tell everybody we're bad or were being bad so we couldn't go to this place or hang with that person. Plus the church firmly believed the verse in the Bible that says to obey your parents in the Lord for this is right. So they wouldn't stick up for us anyway. My aunts went to the church, and they would try to check on us to see how we were doing, but they were always blocked by Greta and the church people. They were met with "They're fine, and we're taking good care of them. You don't need to worry about them. They are in the Lord's hands."

No matter what, I kept my face together though because I believed my life would always be like this, and no one would defend me, love me, or even believe me because she had everyone fooled. I knew I wasn't getting help from them. From a young age, I knew I'm the only person who is going to look out for me. I also knew I had to be strong all the time. I learned how to bury my emotions to survive and endure all the abuse by clicking on a switch when it was happening.

The sexual abuse was happening so often that I became numb from a little girl. It wasn't just Ronald either. There were also members from the church or some of the brothers' friends that stayed with us sometimes. They would make me do things to them. One particular time, Ronald came in my room while I was sleeping, and Derrick was playing in our room, so I didn't think anything of it when I was being awakened. I thought Derrick wanted to play with me. It was Ronald waking me up to abuse me. He laid me on the floor. I had on a skirt and tank top, and he started molesting me while my brother was sitting there playing with the toys. Remember I turn on a switch when I'm being abused, but at that particular time, I couldn't because my brother was right there, and I was too worried about him. He kept his head facing the window and kept playing with his cars, thank goodness. My anger grew at that moment. I couldn't but wanted to try and stop it somehow. My brother was in his own world, which relieved me but made me sad at the same time. Ronald kept saying, "Derrick, I'm using Tina as my pillow, see. I'm going to fall asleep on top of her. She's so comfy." I wanted to murder him. When he was finished, he got up and walked out. Derrick never turned around as he said those things. He just laughed and said okay. I was grateful because he didn't understand.

From all of these guys sexually abusing me, I knew I was a piece of meat. I was on earth to satisfy men's needs. If he didn't care that my brother was there, imagine what he would start to do in the future. This continued until I was fourteen. One day, he just stopped and I don't know why. I was heartbroken when he stopped because I was accustomed to it and looked forward to it because in some twisted way, it made me feel loved and wanted. When he stopped, I thought I gained too much weight or wasn't desirable anymore, and that shattered my self-esteem even more. I looked forward to Ronald touching me by this time. I know you may not understand that or even judge it because you didn't go through it, but this was all my mind and body were accustomed to. It was my form of acceptance and love. When it stopped, I was left with a severe complex about how I looked and if I would be desirable to men because of everything that happened.

We always woke up to the sound of Greta yelling and demanding us to get out of bed and clean and watch the day care kids. My brother, sister, and I were seven, eight, and nine when we started watching the day care. After all the kids went home, we would clean the house from top to bottom every day. We were real-life Cinderella. This was our life every day. It started with abuse and ended with abuse—watching the day care, cleaning, church, physical, emotional, and sexual abuse. This went on for years and years. On the days when we had school, we would clean before we went to school, then clean when we came back home. We were so controlled and abused that we thought everything she said was right and were just too afraid to say anything back. We were also too afraid to fight back and didn't know how to fight back. We also thought the church and their rules were gospel because it was preached to us every day in church and at the house. Greta was manipulative, demonic, and controlling. We were so controlled that even when I left at eighteen, I was still afraid and feared her phone calls. I would tremble when I was on the phone with her. When she would tell us to do something, she always had a demonic smirk on her face. She was pure evil and got tremendous joy out of making our lives hell. We didn't say words because we were in emotional pain and torture, but I believe God knew exactly how we were feeling. A deep hatred was born inside of me for Greta, my life, and everything because we were enduring this and couldn't tell anyone.

When I turned eight, my life would get even worse. My mom had AIDS from being a prostitute, but I never thought she would die. On December 15, 1995, my mom died! Everything that was happening to me was bad, but this was the worst pain in comparison. I was so angry and numb at the same time. It became so intense that I found myself in a place of complete isolation. I was in the world, but my mind, heart, and soul were numb, and I vowed to turn it off and never turn it back on. I was mad at everything and everyone. I was thinking, *Who am I gonna talk to now my momma's gone?*

Even though she couldn't respond, I still talked which helped release some stuff. I was angry because I felt like my mom believed the Word and believed God and what the Word said, and she was never healed! I was angry at the church because I felt like they didn't pray hard enough for her. I felt like she believed, yet why was she not healed, God! I felt like she left us all alone to deal with everything. I was angry at her for dying. I felt she was being selfish, leaving us and going to heaven where she didn't have to deal with pain or anything. I never hated her, but I was jealous and mad that she wasn't enduring life anymore. She was happy and free. I wasn't! The few years before she died she wound up being confined to a hospital bed because she could barely move and wouldn't eat or drink. It was hard to see her like that. She was so skinny. When my siblings and I would go in the room, she would do her best to smile at us. I still would go in there and talk to her about some stuff I was going through. I talked to her about school and just sharing I felt sad today and just shared about my brothers and sister. You may ask why I didn't share my abuse. It's because she could barely talk, and she was in so much pain and barely coherent. I didn't want to put this burden on her. About a month before she died, she would always say she saw angels in her room, and they were ready to take her home. I thought, *They can just heal you rather than take you to heaven.*

On December 15, Greta told my sister to go check on her. My sister did and came back and told her she was sleeping. After a few hours, the nurse came to clean and feed her, but when the nurse saw her, she knew she was dead. She was cold and stiff. When my sister checked on her she was already gone but she didn't know. I don't remember who told me. I just remember crying so hard to the point where every part of my body felt the pain and ache of her leaving. Her funeral was four days later. They had the funeral at the church which my aunts and cousins attended along with the church people. I was sitting on the front row. I cried until I had no tears left in my body. Afterward, we went to bury her. I could not comprehend this in my little mind. We went back to my house for the wake. There were so many people there cooking and cleaning. I was just sitting on the chair numb, staring at everybody. My real aunt and her kids came to visit, but the church people wouldn't let them inside. I remember them actually blocking the door and saying, "They are fine. They have us (meaning the church people) here." They said, "We don't cry in this house, and they will be fine with us. Don't worry."

That was the last time I saw my aunts until I got older and moved out. I remember the look on my aunt's face, the pain and horror she felt. I also remember the look on Greta's face. It was like the sneer of evil. At that moment, I knew our lives were going to get worse, and we would be controlled by Greta for all our days. After they left, Greta turned to me and said, "Stop crying. Enough of those tears. We don't cry in this house" I was shattered in a million pieces. That was the last time I cried.

A day later, Ronald came in to molest me. I cried even though I tried not to. I was thinking, *My mom just died, and you're on top of me already.* I learned how to cope by not feeling anything and biting the skin off my fingers. They would constantly bleed and ache. Some people would cut their arms or legs, mine was biting the skin off my fingers.

Life went on as normal, but then a year later, when I was nine, Daniel died from AIDS. He was four. He was staying with us more in his later years so we could spend as much time with him as we could before he died. Not that we expected him to die, but we knew it was a possibility because he wasn't getting better. Elizabeth always gave him his shots and injections and played and talked with him. She was really close to him. I really felt bad for her when he died. She talked and shared with him the same way I talked and shared with our mom. Of course, she didn't tell him personal stuff. She just shared how her day was and asked him how he was feeling and doing. He was her sounding board and best friend. When he died, I felt like Elizabeth lost a piece of herself. I cried and was hurt, but Elizabeth was so much closer to him than me. It was sudden. We were all on our way to church, and Victoria was holding him. Daniel just closed his eyes and never opened them again. Victoria's eyes turned red, and we all knew he was gone. His funeral was held at the church also. It was small, and they said a few words to talk about his life. They mentioned his beautiful smile, how he would light up a room when he came in, and his enduring spirit. They had the wake at our house again. All I was worried about was my sister. At his funeral, I remember my sister crying so hard. I think a piece of her died that day also. I cried a little at his funeral, but I was so numb at that point that I really didn't feel anything. But my sister though, the look in her eyes was heartbreaking, and it hurt me. When the funeral was over, we buried him and went back to the house for the wake.

After he passed, life went on as usual with chores, the abuse, school, and church. When the oldest son was in the army, sometimes people from the church would stay with us. One of the church members woke me out of my sleep because he squeezed my breast so hard. Before I came to, I thought, *This can't be the oldest son because he's in the army right now, so whose touching me.* After he squeezed my breast, I got up and stared at him. He stared at me with lustful eyes. The next night, he woke me up and had his fingers inside my vagina and made me do other things. It hurt so bad I was walking around limping. This went on for some time because they stayed with us for about five months. A couple of months went by, and Greta's nephew came to stay with us for a couple of days. I woke up because I felt something inside my butt. When I came to, his penis was inside my butt. Victoria woke up to find him on top of me. She told her mom, and he went to jail. Now I know you're asking why I didn't tell her about her son. This is the reason: she worshiped him and thought he could do no wrong no matter what he did. She really loved him a lot and he always did stuff for her, from buying her stuff she wanted to paying the bills. On the other hand, why would I even tell her when she was abusive to us already. Plus, I knew she would not believe me.

One time I saw my sister being abused by a guy from the church, and he was trying to apologize and offered me toys and stuff. I told him I wasn't going to tell anyway because I knew no one would believe me. I still am trying to forgive myself for that to this day. The look on my sister's face was numb just like me. She was used to it.

Over the years, I had many people touch me, plus the years of emotional, physical, and psychological abuse by Greta and Victoria. I was a very numb, quiet, and introverted child who held everything in. On top of everything, we moved like every six months to a year because Greta wasn't making enough money, and the money that she did make she gave it to the church. Now this may seem weird, but I felt a little bad for Greta because they were taking advantage of her also. She would give the church all her money and buy them stuff they said they needed. She would buy them groceries and give into the six different offerings they had. She could not say no, no matter what they asked for. I felt bad for her, but on the other hand, I was like, she's getting what she deserves, but we were suffering because we had no food in the house. I would steal food from the store or anywhere I found some in the house. She would volunteer to pass food around the neighborhood so we would get that food sometimes. I would steal the bread and stuff from other bags and hide it in our room. I would steal anything I could get from the store. I got beat for it, but I did not care. I was hungry, and it was kind of a way to have control in my life, if that makes sense. Stealing was something I had control over. It was my form of taking back what little power I had.

When I was getting abused one time, he tried to lay me down and I was refusing and he said, "You might as well give in because you're not going to be able to stop me." I knew he was right. I was like, *Just go on ahead and let him do it and get it over with.* For the first time, he tried to tongue kiss me over and over, and I said in my head, *He's going too far now.* As if the other stuff weren't too far. I was abused since I was four, and I was fourteen now, so by this time, I was pretty trained on what to expect. As I mentioned earlier, I also realized I was enjoying it by then. It was all I knew, and it was my foundation. My emotions and the sexual part of me was looking forward to it, and I hated myself so much for that. I'm going to try and explain it. It's like my body craved it, and I liked when it was happening because some form of me felt wanted in a way, even though it was perverted. Let me make sure I mention Nicholas never ever touched us. He always looked out for us. Ronald and Nicholas had pornographic magazines that

I discovered by accident because I was cleaning the basement. I taught myself how to masturbate, and it felt good. When I was not being abused, I could use this as a form of arousal, comfort, and pleasure. Even though I wasn't in control of my life, when I masturbated, it felt like I gained a little piece back because I was in control of how I wanted my arousal to be. I felt dirty, but I liked it at the same time because it made my emotions and body feel good. At this time, I relied even more on the pornographic magazines and my masturbation to fulfill the sexual desire that was awoken prematurely inside of me. It also filled the loneliness I felt for a little while. About three years later, I sent Ronald a letter stating,

> I remember everything you did to me and all the years of abuse and torture I went through with you. You could have given me a break once or looked out for us once. You just let my sister, brother, and I get abused by you, your sister, and your mom for years. What kind of a man are you? You constantly abused us and gave no regard to our feelings, emotions, or anything. You just wanted to fulfill your sexual desires. I forgive you. I'm just angry and hurt.

I said I forgive him even though I didn't go through any type of counseling or therapy. I realized I had not actually forgiven him yet. I was just taught to say that. He sent me a letter back saying he didn't think I remembered the abuse. I wanted to strangle him! I was still living with the foster lady, and his letter came with all her other bills. My heart stopped for a minute because I thought she was going to read it. She never did though. She just said, "Tina, you have a letter."

Now I know that was God. You must understand that she reads and was in control of everything. I know that was God when she didn't open the letter. My response to his letter was, *How could you not think I would remember that?* I just thought those thoughts in my head. I didn't send another letter to him.

As I got older—I'm gonna try and explain this—I felt the trauma and pain in my heart, bones, and body. It was like the trauma had manifested and grown in my body as I got older. All throughout my childhood and teens, when me, Ronald, or anybody saw each other, we pretended like nothing was happening, and everything was normal, whether we went out to eat with the family or shopping or anything. We all pretended like nothing was happening behind the scenes. I asked him how the army was and if he has any friends. He would answer and vice versa.

About once a month, Greta was nice, which made me try hard to be on her good side. How we knew she was going to be nice that day was she would wake us up nice and say something like, "Good morning. I've prepared pancakes and stuff for y'all. Come and have some." Then she would be nice and make our plates and say we can watch movies and go outside. I knew this was only going to last for one day, but I treasured it.

One of these nice days, she said Elizabeth and I could have a sleepover. Greta invited some of the girls from the church to come over. I was so scared and frozen at this sleepover I couldn't even enjoy it. I was scared because I was feeling so much shame from all the abuse. My thoughts were *What if the girls see the abuse that we go through? They will never talk to us again.* Or *What if they think we're weird?* I was holding onto shame, fear, and embarrassment for my family and myself. One of the girls actually said, "This house seems so cold." I didn't say anything, but I knew exactly what she meant. I didn't enjoy the sleepover at all and couldn't wait for it to be over. As I got older, I realized she did this right before the social workers came to check on us. It was a strategy to say she was nice, and we're doing okay. I still wanted her to like me, even though I knew it was impossible. So I played along. I wanted to be loved so bad. I also wanted to feel something other than pain, so I found it through porn and magazines. When I was in the sixth grade, I had my graduation, and Greta never came. I was so heartbroken and devastated because I wanted someone to be there for me—even if it was her.

When I turned fifteen, my brother, sister, and I were officially adopted. Even though we lived with the lady since we were four, the process took a long time for us to get adopted. The social worker asked us if we wanted to be adopted by this lady or if we wanted to live with someone else. By this time, I was so scared of Greta that I just nodded my head, along with Derrick and Elizabeth. I should have screamed *no!* But it was the only home I knew, and I thought, *What if I go somewhere else, and it's worse?* So I nodded my head in agreement. I was comfortable because I knew somewhat the abuse that was coming. So we stayed.

Elizabeth, Derrick, and I were officially adopted when we were fifteen, sixteen, and seventeen. Around this time, I became a little defiant. I would talk back or say stuff under my breath and completely ignore her when she started fussing or screaming. I would start humming, singing, or tuning her out. I didn't care. I was like, *What's the worse she could do to me that she has not done to me already?* Her favorite thing when we were older was her kicking us out or saying "You guys can leave." She knew we didn't have anywhere to go though, which was torture in itself.

Our lives were pretty much the same after that. We did our usual cleaning all day and night and going to church six or seven days a week. My existence was a zombie at this point. I just went through the routine of doing what we were told. When I was seventeen, I finally graduated from high school in May of 2006.

By this time, most of the people I had known left the church. I didn't know it at the time, but they left because of all the mistreatment that was happening, from them taking offerings six different times to the people with jobs paying for other people's conferences and bills. The teachers that taught us were not being paid, so they were poor and constantly giving the money they eventually got back into the church. We still couldn't wear pants or listen to music that was not Christian based as they call it. I believe, at first, when the church opened, they were definitely trying to follow God and doing the right thing by trying to lead the people to God. They had the best of intentions, but I believe if your heart and mind are not constantly seeking God or if you're not working on your character, then you can be led astray. I feel like that's what happened to them. The congregation held on to the apostle's and pastors' words as gold. They looked at them like they were God and followed their leading no matter how it sounded. Unfortunately, I was a part of that too I felt like they were right, and I tried to follow everything they said. I knew deep in my heart that God cannot be about sexual, physical, emotional, or psychological abuse or people living one way in the church's eyes but coming home and being a completely different person. This cannot be God. I wanted to follow God, and I was thinking they knew the way, so I brushed my concerns, fears, and worries aside constantly because I wanted to be a good daughter for God.

Before my senior graduation, we had a small dinner celebration at a restaurant with the other graduate and I, along with the pastor. It was actually really nice. I was an hour late because I was getting ready, but when I got there, it was really nice. They had flowers and gifts for us. They wished us well on our journey. We didn't have a prom. Our school was so small that we didn't have enough people in each grade to have one.

I made it to the day of my graduation. The church was there, the apostle, pastor, and some of the church members. Two of us graduated as seniors that day. Greta was there, and honestly, I didn't care if she came or not. My brother and sister were there, so that was really exciting. We had a small ceremony where both of us walked down the aisle and got handed our diplomas. The weeks before the ceremony, we made these sort of graduation books to commemorate our time at the school. It was actually really fun. It had all of our experiences in it, from us laughing to telling jokes to schoolwork and just hanging out. To this day, I still don't know what happened to that book. There were some good memories in there. Despite that, I was ready to get out of there. I didn't know what I was going to do with my life yet. I didn't even know if I was going to be able to leave because Greta forbade it. She had such control I didn't even realize I'm grown I could just leave if I wanted. (I don't wish that type of mind control on anyone, not even my worst enemy.) The ceremony was over, and we all went home. We didn't go out to celebrate or anything. One of the church people was trying to take me out, but Greta was like, "No, we need to go home." So that was my graduation. It was a ceremony, then home.

About five months leading to my graduation, I felt like, *I'm going to kill this lady if you don't get me out of here*. I never said this out loud to God or anyone at the time. It was just my thoughts. I kept thinking, *I can't do this anymore. I'm gonna lose whatever piece of my mind I have left. I'm dying, God!* I built a prison in my mind where no one could get in, and I couldn't get out. The prison was all the horrible thoughts I thought about myself—the verbal, mental, sexual, and physical abuse I received from Greta, Ronald, and the guys. My mind lived there and was tormented every hour of every day. Out of the blue, one of the ladies in the church asked if I would be interested in going to the school at this church that we visited every year. I casually said yes, but on the inside, it was a big *yes*! I didn't want to get too happy because I didn't know if it was actually going to happen. I had little hope that I could go. God went to work.

Chapter 4

A Glimmer of Hope

Every year, the church would attend a Christian conference in Florida. I don't know how they heard about it. This was where all the prophets (people that hear the voice of God) and apostles (men or women that led the people closer to God) gathered to be empowered, activated, and prayed over. I loved it there. I always felt peace and the love of God when I went there. The bishop who was over the whole church was a great, kind, and strong man of God. He was activated in prophecy from a young age, and then from there, he helped facilitate churches in different regions and states around the world. He completely and selflessly gave his whole heart and life to God. I loved the church because they taught you how to hear God's voice and search him out for yourself. We went there every year since I was little.

One of the members of the church I was attending told me they also have a school for theology (the study of God). I needed something, and I know God knew I needed to get out of the situation I was in. These comments were only thoughts in my head. I never dreamed or thought about God listening to me or answering my inner thoughts. A couple of days passed, and the lady from the church bought it up to the apostle one Sunday after church. He talked to me about it, asking if I wanted to go. I said, "Yes, I do." And it would be a great opportunity to learn more about God and the Holy Spirit. Of course, my secret reasons were to get away from Greta and the church as a whole. He agreed and said I should go.

Then he went to Greta and shared, "I think Tina should go to the school to learn and grow more within herself and within God. It will be great for her."

In my heart, I knew she was going to say no. On the other hand, I knew the apostle had control over all their thoughts, minds, and actions, so I had a glimmer of hope that she would say yes. She just said okay. She wasn't happy or enthused about it. I know she let me go because the apostle said I should. I know it killed her, but I was ecstatic on the inside. Still I was not about to get too happy until my foot stepped inside the school thousands of miles away. I knew God was at work because she never let me out of her sight, let alone think of me moving thousands of miles away. God was truly at work because everyone agreed. Greta still was herself with her comments and remarks, but with the knowledge of me going away, it just didn't bother me because I had something to look forward to. I still can't believe it as I'm writing this.

Around the middle of August, we all had a meeting in the apostle's office. They shared with me to continue following God, not to get into worldly things, meaning music, dressing, and going out. They shared they would pay my tuition, but I needed to work also. They prayed a lot over me which I appreciated because I was excited, but I was still a tiny bit nervous because it was something I never experienced before. They also shared if I needed any-thing, I shouldn't hesitate to ask. They will provide it. For the month of August, I packed and prayed that I was still going. The month dragged by, but the end finally came.

In the beginning of September, I was all ready to leave. I thought so much about leaving my sister and brother behind. I felt a huge knot inside of me because they would be left to deal with all her craziness and demonic ways. I felt bad but couldn't stay there anymore. I had to leave. It was one of the hardest things because I love them so much, and I knew my actions would cause them even more heart-ache, but I felt it was time. And with how everything lined up, I knew it was God, and it was the right thing to do.

The day came for me to move, and I remember the sky was so beautiful and clear. The atmosphere of the house was somber. No one really said anything the whole day. We went to Sunday service earlier that day. The apostle and members of the church all put their hands on me and prayed over me. The apostle prophesied over me (spoke the words of the Lord over my life). He gave me the tapes of the prophecy. I looked around the church and the mem-bers and took it all in. The fact that I wasn't going to see them for a while and the fact that these were the people I grew up with, I didn't feel any pain. I just felt I was going to miss some of them. I was ready to go. I saw the pain in Elizabeth's eyes. Greta didn't really say anything either. She was in her room most of the day. I brought all of my stuff to the front door. Three of the ladies volunteered to drive me down to the school. They came to my house and helped me load the van we were using. I looked around the house one last time and couldn't wait to leave even more. Greta said nothing but helped put a few items in the van. I was surprised. I said goodbye to my brother and sister. I can still feel the pain of that moment as I write this. I knew my brother was going to be okay because he was happy 90 percent of the time. I was worried about my sister. She looked completely numb and in such pain. I wanted to hold her so bad. I just had to let her go and trust she was going to be okay. The three ladies and I backed out of the driveway and drove away. I didn't take my eyes off my sister and brother. We turned, and that was the last time I saw them for a while. I was able to call them because Ronald bought me a cell phone before I left. Out of her children, I only missed Nicholas because he treated us right.

The road trip was actually fun. I bought books, magazines, and music to listen to on my CD player while they drove. We didn't really talk that much. They just asked if I was nervous and excited to go and just reminded me of what the apostle said. Other than that, they talked among themselves, and I kept to myself. We stopped occasionally for gas and food. Each of the ladies drove about eight hours. It took about twenty-four hours to reach the destination. We arrived just in time for registration at the school. We went inside the church, and they gave them the money they raised for my tuition. It wasn't enough, but the school accepted without hesitation. They gave me the rules and regulations for the school, and I met some of the staff.

Pinch me; I could not believe I was actually here. After we met everyone, they drove me to the house I would be staying at. It was me and three other girls.

The house was huge and beautiful. We had our own rooms with connecting bathrooms. My room consisted of two twin beds decorated with flowers. I had a huge tan dresser, closet, and a TV. I loved it because it was my first real exposure to freedom. My roommates were really nice too and asked me where I was from and how I am. I don't recall being too scared because I was by myself. I was more of taking in my environment, observing everything, and I was still surprised all of the church members were in agreement and shocked this actually happened. The three ladies who drove me stayed for a few days to make sure I was okay, then they drove back to Jersey.

The next day was orientation. This day was a short day. We got to meet some of our teachers and went over the curriculum. After that, we left until the next day. I tell you, when you're desperate, and your heart is in the right place, God will answer you. There were about twenty to thirty people in my class. The school consisted of first-year (which I was), second-year, and third-year students. It's sort of like a church school, but the teachings are all about God, and they go deep into making sure you're healed. They train you on how to hear his voice and getting healed from what you've gone through or may have gone through before you got there. Some of the classes are theology, prophetic training, healing, and worship. I loved it because I always wanted to understand God and understand why I had to go through the things I went through. We got out around three, and as soon as we left, one of the students dropped me off at home.

I started walking to places near me, looking for anyone who would hire me. I did find a job rather quickly. They hired me on the spot. It was a place called Moe's Southwest Grill, which is like a Mexican restaurant. I started the next day. I went to school in the morning and worked at night. The job was about a mile from my house, so I was able to walk to and from work every day. The next day, we had our first official class.

We had a worship and prayer session, then we all dispersed to our separate areas, divided by our year—first-, second-, and third-year students. My first class was Bible, sort of like learning who you are and why God created you to be on this earth. It was a good class, and we delved deeply into the Bible. I was still too shy and scared to say anything, so I didn't ask questions that year, but I enjoyed listening to other people's questions and answers. We had Bible and some other classes that day. I don't really remember all of them.

I had two amazing friends in particular who looked out for me and always invited me to stuff and made sure I was okay. They were godsent! All three of us hung out and did a lot of stuff together that I never really did. For instance, we went out to eat, talked about our feelings, went to the movies, and just did fun stuff. It was one of the best and scariest years. It was great because I was away but scary because Greta still had control over me.

I was thinking when I moved, it would be an automatic change, and I would be free—not so! I remember I was in my fourth month of school, and she called me. One of her rules/control things was that she needed to know where I was at all times.

So that time, I forgot to call her, and she called me, saying, "I told you to call me no matter what you're doing. You think you're grown now? I will come up there and get you right now. I still have control over what you do, so you do what I tell you."

This was what she said among other things. Mind you, I didn't realize I was a grown woman yet and could do what I want. I still had that same fear and control over me that I had since I was a little girl. After she said that to me, I just walked into class like nothing happened. This was a part of my life for the first year of school. No one knew. I always pretended everything was okay mainly because I didn't think anyone cared, and I really didn't know how to express my feelings. I was a pro at wearing a mask.

The school had great teachers. My favorite one was our theology teacher. He was extremely insightful and taught us so many things about the stories in the Bible and what God meant with the parables he wrote to us. One of the classes we went through was like a soul (mind, will, and emotions) healing class. It was a three-part series that started with you acknowledging all the feelings you feel right now and all the feelings you felt as you were going through some of the traumatic things in your life, whether it's hate, anger, selfishness, jealousy, or anything you feel and just want to share. We started by sharing with each other, or if we're not comfortable, we shared with only one person. We also had journals that we wrote in. The journaling helped a lot. I felt like I could express a lot more writing than actually talking. As we were sharing in whatever form we're comfortable with, they encouraged us to acknowledge it and see how the feelings were controlling our life and not allowing us to be free. We also discussed healing and mechanisms we can use to get healed. It was mainly the journaling and praying a lot, which helped. Around this time, I was really emotionally captive and didn't realize it. I was thinking I was being healed and free, but I wasn't because as I shared, I was also numb to what I had been through. As I shared, I would share like, "Yes, I was sexually abused. I'm good though. I prayed and talked to God about it, and now I'm healed." I sounded just like how I was trained to sound by the church I grew up in. I didn't realize there were layers to this, and I was still really numb and traumatized. Don't get me wrong. All levels of sharing are good because you get to see where you are in your healing. For me, I just didn't realize I was still so numb and hurt.

The second step consisted of us saying the hurt out loud or in whispers. We say the person's name and say we forgive them. You won't feel like you forgive them right then, but you keep saying it until you're able to see them and not feel the feelings you felt before you did the course. It's a day-by-day process. It was a great course, and it helped me to see where I was and what I needed to work on inside of me. Still it was years until I was actually able to confront the abuse, pain, anger, loneliness, depression, rage, and hurt. You know what else I learned over the years while you're carrying anger over the people that abused you? They are living their lives not thinking about you. Trust me; it will take a while to be healed and learn how to forgive and let go, but *don't give up*! It will get easier, and you will be able to do it, if you do the work. Even to this day, I'm still learning this is not a one-, five-, or ten-year journey; it's a lifetime. My first year of schooling was done. It was a great year.

When we were finished, I found out I had to go back to New Jersey for the summer. I was terrified because I felt like all the progress I made during that year will be stripped away by Greta and her demonic ways. I felt like I was a person going back in the lion's den to be killed. I knew I was gonna need to fight my thoughts and stuff on the inside because she would try with all her might to try and have some type of control over me. The day came, and I got on the plane, then I landed in Jersey. The summer turned out to be full of fighting and pleasant surprises. I got to the house and she just said hi and that was it, then she walked back to her room and closed the door. I didn't have huge expectations, so that was good for me. I was so happy to see my brother. He was so happy to see me. My sister was staying with another lady in the church, so I didn't see her until later. It was so good seeing Elizabeth. I held her for a long time.

The next day, Greta went back to her same self. She was so evil she was saying and doing everything she could to get rid of the change that happened inside of me. She would just say stuff like, "You're not changed. You're going to always be dumb and stupid." "You will never be anything. Just because you went to that school doesn't mean

I still don't have control over you." Or "I can always make you stay here and never leave."

Every day it was something, whether it was yelling or making me clean or just saying evil things. *It was hell!* She was definitely killing my spirit. I felt like I did all of this work in the school, only for it to be stripped away. I got a job at Family Dollar for the summer, so that was a little relief. I wasn't in the house for eight hours. I was feeling like a failure, and the depression and hatred of myself were definitely getting to me.

About two months of being home, we were in church on Sunday. The apostle was praying over some of the members. Then he called me up to the front and said clearly, "Don't let nothing or no one steal what God has placed in your heart and mind. He led you to that school for a reason. He did not put all that work in you for it to be robbed out of you."

I tell you I felt the presence of God on me. It was amazing, and I just cried and cried. It was a warm presence, and I could not stand up. It was so strong. I just so happen to look up while I was crying, and Greta was looking like a pure demon. Her face was indescribable. I felt like this lady will never change, and she will never want me to be happy or loved. I felt such a release knowing that and being able to move on with my life. I promised myself it will not be taken away again.

After church, the apostle and the pastor called me in the office to tell me I was going back to school in Florida. I will be taking a bus back. I tell you, if there was such a thing as bursting out of your skin with excitement, I was the picture of it! I was determined to get through the next two months without losing myself. She was still her same way over the next few months, but it didn't bother me as much as it did when I first got there because I was going back, and I promised myself I was not going to let her get to me.

A couple of weeks later, Greta called me downstairs to ask me if her son ever touched me. I said yes. She threw a glass at me and said, "I don't believe you."

I told her, "It's true, and that's why I never told you because I knew you wouldn't believe me."

I cried because of the anger I felt. I just went to my room. I don't know how long I stayed there. Now I was wondering because my first thought was how did she even know? I never told anyone besides God and maybe a couple of people at the school. I found out she found my sister's diary and started reading it, and she showed it to the people at the church saying she was lying, and she doesn't believe her. Then that's when she came and asked me and I told her he touched me too. The next day, she took me to the pastor and apostle and told them what happened. They asked me if it was true and if it happened to my sister. I went out of the office and asked my sister if it happened to her. Of course, she said yes, plus I knew it happened to her because I would wake up to find guys on top of her and there was the guy I caught touching her. She shared with me she saw guys sexually abusing me also. For some reason, we never voiced it to each other. Saying it out loud gives it a different feel and perspective, making it real. I went back in the office and told them it happened to her too. I told them I forgive him, and I'm okay. Greta never mentioned or talked about it again. I honestly don't know why, and I'm okay with not knowing. I really wasn't, but I just said it. I was mad at the church because they didn't do anything or try to help. I also knew there was nothing they could do, and they wouldn't help me anyway. I knew I shouldn't be mad because they didn't have the thought process to call DCF or anything. I was mad though and wanted them to do something even though I didn't say anything. I felt like they didn't care because as I shared before, they were the type of church that followed the Bible relentlessly and believed everything that happened in the home or at church should be left in those places. My anger came to a head again. I didn't show it though. They just said okay, and the meeting was over. I determined in my heart that day that I wasn't coming back. I didn't know how that was going to happen, but all I know is I wasn't coming back no matter what.

The day finally came when I was going back to Florida. I said my goodbyes to everyone, hopped on the bus, and I was gone. *Yippee!* I was extremely happy and grateful to God. The relief was immense. I was on the bus for three days. Then I finally made it, and one of the students came to pick me up. He took me to the school to register, and then we went to the apartments where I was going to live. It was so nice. There were three of us staying in a six-bed-room house. There was Ceila, Ebony, and I. We each had two rooms and our own bathroom.

I met Ceila first. She was really nice. Little did I know she would help me change a lot from the inside out. I met

Ebony later. She wanted to stay with her parents for the night. I immediately went to go look for a job in the area because I still couldn't drive yet. I was walking up the street, and Ceila happened to be out and picked me up and took me around to look for jobs. I wound up back at Moe's, the same job I had when I started my first year. I started the next day. It was great. I cooked, cleaned, and took orders. I was promoted to assistant manager within five months. I still was awkward, weird, and somewhat quiet. I still only wore dresses or skirts, ankle length or longer. I look back and can't believe I wore that while I was working. I loved my boss. She was sweet and did everything she could to help make sure I understood the job.

The next day was orientation, and I was happy to see all the students that I went to school with last year were back. We met and introduced ourselves to the first-year students. They had the same nervous look all of us had our first year. We welcomed them with open arms. The classes were almost the same except we went deeper into our lives in the second year. If I can describe the feelings I felt, it was amazing that I had the privilege of being there again and away from Greta and everyone else. Then after that, we went home.

Ceila was great. She always dropped me off and picked me up from work. Ceila and I got close over the year unexpectedly. We talked about our lives in detail. I told her about Greta, the church, and all the men who sexually abused me. It was actually really helpful. I shared a lot, and she just talked and listened. She listened and encouraged me to talk about it when I felt angry or hurt or disappointed. It was

56

hard for me to share, but I tried anyway. I really appreciate her and God putting her in my life because she helped me see a lot of stuff. For instance, I didn't need to stay on the phone as Greta verbally abused me. I didn't need to take her mess. I was free now, and I didn't live there. The logic didn't occur to me that I didn't need to sit on the phone and take the abuse. I guess when you're in something so long, you don't realize you are actually free and have choices. She also shared I didn't need to wear just skirts. I could wear pants and other items to show my beautiful skin. I remember when I first started riding with her, I told her she listened to worldly music, and she just calmly said I could listen to whatever music I like. I was like, "That is so true, and realized I can do that also." I was slowly but surely realizing how controlled I had been and realizing I have the power to be free. I was becoming free, I tell you, and it was a different feeling because I never thought I could truly be free. That idea didn't cross my mind.

Ceila was honest and herself twenty-four seven. It helped me to let some of my walls down that I built up for over eighteen years. I was a whole mess. I would act out and have fits of being angry, sarcastic, or just mean. I didn't realize my trauma was spilling over into other areas of my life. Ceila got the brunt of it because we were becoming close, so we argued a lot, but for the most part, we came back together and talked about it. We wound up getting closer and closer by going through stuff together and just learning about life together. At this point, I didn't realize it, but I was so desperate for love and someone to just accept me I was willing to do anything they wanted to do because

I always thought people would leave unless I did what they wanted to do or behaved like they wanted me to behave. (So sad that someone has thoughts or behaviors like that because we're afraid of not being loved and accepted.) And unfortunately, despite having my roommate, the school, and God, I was still constantly tormented from thoughts of "I will never be loved or liked" or "No one will want to be my friend." I didn't love myself, and I needed to love myself first. I didn't see or understand that until years later. Overall, my second year was amazing. I continued to grow and have different mindsets about things.

When Christmas came my second year, Ceila asked if I wanted to go to her house. For the first time, I didn't go back to Jersey, and I was surprised and happy that Ceila even wanted me to come. I mean we were close, but I still had the fear that she didn't really like me, a fear that I still struggle with to this day. I met her family who were wonderful. They always made sure I was okay and checked on me while I stayed there. I was a quiet observer. I rarely talked, so I just watched how they interacted. I loved their interaction. It was little things like laughing at each other's jokes, going to parties, going to family functions, and hanging out with one another—these are things I didn't experience, so for me, it was a breath of fresh air. They simply enjoy each other's company. These were some of the things that made me cry a couple of times alone because I wished I had a true family. I highly enjoyed when they told me stories about them growing up and how they would have cousin sleepovers and all the aunts and uncles would be playing cards while they played together. I also enjoyed hearing stories about them growing up and being together. I loved it and always wished I had a family like that. I'm still amazed at them to this day because they took me in without hesitation, and they took care of me with no motives or wanting anything from me. I love and appreciate each and every one of them! Thank you, guys, for being you. It means so much more than I can express with words!

Going to Ceila's house for Christmas was the first decision I made with freedom. The church and Greta made a fuss about it, saying I shouldn't be with them for they are not of God. I should be with the church because they knew what's best for me, that I was following the devil now. These were just some of the things they would share. I just told them "I'm going to my roommate's house for Christmas." I said I didn't know if they're of God. But I was still going because I knew it was them trying to control me but in a questionable way. I believe Greta knew she didn't have control of me after that because I learned not to pick up her calls or anything.

Christmas break was over, and back to school we went. Before we went back to school, I asked Ceila's parents if I could stay for the summer, and they said yes. The second half was just like the first with school and work. On summer break, I went to live with my roommate. It was a great summer. After that, we went back to school for our third year. I felt like I grew a lot over the past two years. I had the ability and freedom to make decisions without being afraid of what anyone would think. I felt a little bit more freedom in my soul. I was ready to conquer my emotions and thoughts this year.

In December of my third year, Ceila told me she was moving back home because she felt like she got what she came for. I understood that even though I was gonna miss her a lot because she was part of the reason I was free now. I kind of felt like I would lose that ability now that she was leaving. I knew I couldn't rely on her because I'm the one who found the freedom inside of me and with the help of everyone, especially God and me not picking up the phone. I knew I could do it. I needed to press forward and not lean or depend on her. I was sad but ready at the same time. I knew I had grown to a point where I didn't need a crutch. So off Ceila went, and there I stayed. The rest of the year was kind of the same. I grew as a person a lot, and I was actually happy for the first time. I made great friendships and memories with these people. One of my classmates taught me how to drive, and I officially got my license when I was twenty-one.

Chapter 5

A New Life

In May 2009, I was officially done with school. It was a great three years, but I was ready to explore different things. I felt I should stay at the church for another year until I figure out what I was going to do next. I rented a place from one of the church people and lived there while going to church and working. When the year came to a close, I was wondering what was next. I talked to Ceila's parents and asked them if I could live there, and they said yes. Thank God because I could not go back and live in that toxic environment. Remember what I shared earlier. I wasn't going back to Jersey. I didn't know how that was gonna happen, but look at that opportunity that opened up wide. I got a job at a hotel where I would stay for eight years. This was the year everything changed.

In 2010, I wound up cutting everyone off—all the church people, Greta, and even my own siblings. It was one of the hardest things I ever did. I missed my sister and brother so much, but it needed to be done because I still had a lot of the toxic traits and thinking from Greta that needed to be dealt with without the distractions. I needed to cut everyone off so they won't be in my head or saying evil things to me. I needed to be free and be healed. I know you may ask why I cut off my brother and sister. This is the reason: I mentioned earlier that I had a lot of trauma from what I went through. I was angry, mad, yelling, argumentative, and most of the time, I didn't realize my trauma had spilled over into other areas of my life. The stuff that came out of me was toxic, so Celia and I got in a lot of fights over that. Elizabeth was the same way, even though she didn't realize it either. I wanted and was determined to keep my healing, so that meant cutting everyone off who would prevent that. It was hard, but I was determined.

I got a lot of heat and hate for that, from the church people to Greta, everybody feeling like I should come home to be with my family and the church people. I got some text messages and voice mails. Some of them said I'm disobeying God by moving away and cutting everyone off. I'm being used by the devil! I'm not following God anymore. I have demons in me. I'm not obeying Greta. I'm not in God anymore.

I know they were just trying to control me and my movements. This was why I didn't tell anyone where I lived. I was also afraid that they were going to come and find me and take me back to live with them. This was the best thing I ever did for myself and my state of mind. It was hard not talking to Elizabeth and Derrick, but I had to do it for my sanity. I continued to find myself. I wore pants, shorts, dresses, and tank tops. I listened to other music besides Christian music. I got to see what life was like without the church or anyone's input. I was becoming a real person and not a robot. I could not go back to no freedom and being controlled. I had a taste of being loved, and I wanted more. I even changed my phone number.

About a year later, I called my sister and brother and told them how I was doing. My sister was mad at me for not calling her, but I explained, and I think she somewhat understood even though she was hurt. I shared with her my feelings and doubts. We started talking almost every day after that. I didn't talk to Greta that much, just on occasion because she still had my brother. I had to play nice in a way to talk to him. I hated that part. I gritted it though because I needed to speak to him and see how he was doing under her care. My heart ached to get him out. I didn't talk to the church that much. I still felt a connection to some of them, so I would talk to some of them periodically.

I continued to live with Ceila's parents until 2012 when we found an apartment together. For the most part, it was great, and we got along. We lived together for about six years. During the last two years, it was okay. We argued a lot and didn't get along. I believe it was because I was going through so much in my heart, and I was stubborn in a way and wanted things done my way. I was really quiet, so I didn't say how I really felt with certain situations, and then when I was really mad, I would explode and say how I felt which was not healthy at all. You remember I shared earlier I was so desperate for someone to love or like me that I was willing to just go with the flow of anything and not saying stuff that I wanted to do. I didn't realize at the time that I was doing most of the stuff that other people wanted me to do or listening to their advice despite feeling I was contradicting what they said. I didn't realize until later that I was operating out of a feeling that no one would like me or love me if they knew me. I was determined to speak my mind and say how I felt. I'm still learning this now. After those six years, we went our separate ways. I stayed in that apartment we got together, and she moved out. I am extremely grateful for her and the growing pains we had. Ceila helped me grow in a lot of ways and helped me find myself. She also helped me get a taste of real freedom. I'm realizing people are placed in your life for a reason, whether it be a lesson, a teacher, a friend, or just to help you grow at a certain point in your life. Everything is a lesson, and I'm continually in school every day. I am still close to her family, and I'm always at the family functions, movies, and anything else they had.

In 2016, I finally had the courage to return to New Jersey after seven years. This would really determine how much I grew and if these same people would have an impact on my growth and if I actually changed. My sister and I talked all the time I was gone, but I didn't see her for all that time. This was a reunion eight years in the making, and I was looking forward to it. I was a little nervous though because I hadn't seen anyone in about eight years. Off I went to visit Elizabeth and Derrick.

When I pulled up to the house, she came running out to hug me. It was the longest hug. When I walked in the house, Greta was the first one that saw me, and she turned white. She didn't know I was coming, and neither did my brother. When Derrick saw me, he almost cried.

He hugged me for a long time and just kept saying I missed you, I missed you. Greta looked like a ghost and hardly said anything besides "hi" and "how have you been." She knew she had no more control over me. By then I was completely calm myself. I told her I was good, and my life was good. She only asked me surface stuff which was a relief. Then she called some people from the church and told them I was there. They FaceTimed her, and I talked to some of them for a little bit. I also saw Victoria who kept laughing for no reason. She was nervous. I stayed in a hotel for the first week and a half I was there, then I decided to stay at Greta's house for two nights so I can see my brother more. My brother was highly controlled. It was really bad. My heart ached so bad. From the time he woke up until the time he went to bed, he cleaned and worked and worked. He cleaned the house, helped her with stuff she was doing at the church, then came back and cleaned the house again. It was like that for him every day besides when he went to work. I know my brother was happy because that's just his personality, but at times, he would call me and tell me all the stuff Greta did to him. That was one of the hardest things living away because I couldn't rescue him. That was my next mission, to get him out to live with me. I didn't realize at the time I could just take him with me. I was thinking Greta had guardianship over him, so there was no way I could get him. I was also afraid to take him because I was scared of her in that aspect and how she would retaliate, if she would try and hurt him or try and go to the police and say I kidnapped him. I was sort of afraid also because I didn't know how to take care of him if I did get him. And I didn't have a job that pays much, so how would I help him? For the next couple of days I was there, I spent as much time with my brother and sister as I could. I went to visit the church once. I don't know why I did. I guess it was familiar, and they weren't out of my system yet. I did want to see some of the people who went there because they were in the church but weren't like some of the church people.

My visit was coming to a close. I was getting really sad because I was leaving Derrick and Elizabeth. Those last few hours, we said goodbye to each other a whole lot. Then I headed for the airport and was off, headed back to Florida to live in my apartment. For the next three years, I continued to get closer and closer to my brother and sister. I tried to make sure I went to visit whenever I had the opportunity. It was always a great experience going to visit my sister and brother. I didn't go back to visit the people at the church. My brother kept telling me stuff Greta did to him which made me determined to get him out even more.

In the beginning of 2019, I was on Facebook, and I messaged my biological aunt that I wanted to meet my real family. I don't know what made me do this. I believe it's because I had a deep hole inside of me that wouldn't go away. I have not spoken to her in almost sixteen years. But I found her and told her, and she was so excited. She told all of my biological family that my brother, sister, and I were coming to meet them. It was one of the best feelings ever. It was like my life was coming full circle. I talked to my aunt a lot. We had really good conversations about how she grew up, how I grew up. I was able to ask her questions about my mom and the kind of person she was. She always said she was happy and loving and just made some bad decisions. She also shared that she wanted to get us, but Greta was in my mom's ear and telling her we should come live with her. She shared that she tried with all her might to get us, but she wasn't able to. She wasn't because Greta had complete control over us and my mom. Whenever they tried to visit us, she or the church people would stand at the door preventing them from coming in or seeing us. I don't blame my biological family at all because I know they tried to get us but couldn't. I started talking to her more and more. One of the best feelings is finding someone who understands you and what you're feeling because they went through the exact same thing. I shared my feelings with her, and she let me know I'm not crazy a lot of times when I thought I was losing my mind or just weird. I love and appreciate her very much. We set a date, May 2019.

I was extremely nervous but excited. I could not wait to meet my family and get to know them. About two months earlier, my brother called me upset and told me another thing Greta did to him. I told him, "Derrick, you don't have to stay there. You can come live with me. You do not have to deal with her craziness anymore."

So that's what he did. When I came down, we decided he's going to come back and live with me in Florida. He told her he was moving with me, and she kicked him out right away. Thank God my sister had an apartment. He moved in with her until I arrived. Even though she kicked him out, I was happy that he was out because he could sleep without the yelling and abuse. He literally had two months of peace, and I know she regretted doing that because she had no one to help her do anything.

The date finally came to meet my real family. I flew down and stayed at my sister's apartment. The next day, we met at my cousin's house. Nervous doesn't even describe accurately how I felt. I was so scared and excited at the same time. I rode with my sister and brother. All three of us had the same nervous energy. We walked in the house, and most of our family were there ready to greet us. They were so loving. They hugged us all so tight. I cried on the inside, and I'm also crying as I'm typing this. The best way to describe this feeling was like home and warmth. It was one of the best things that happened to me. We talked for a while, and they told me all about my mom and how they grew up. I tell you I felt so loved. It was one amazing night. We talked and talked and got to know each other. I got to meet some of my nieces, nephews, aunts, uncles, and my beautiful grandma. It was beautiful, and it helped heal my heart in a way. The next day, we all met at another cousin's house, and we got to meet even more of our family. After all the meeting, we took a million pictures and exchanged phone numbers. Then we went back to my sister's apartment and talked about everything that happened. We talked to our family one more time before it was time for Derrick and I to go back to Florida. We spent more time with Elizabeth before flying back. I finally had Derrick after years of praying and hoping and wondering if it would ever happen. He was finally free, and he came to live with me. He started experiencing stuff he never experienced like the fair, going to a ton of different stores and buying what he wants, and hanging out with great family. He is so much happier and thriving in his new environment. I call my biological family every now and then to see how they're doing.

To get free, it was an ugly battle that consisted of tears, breaking down many times, being crazy sometimes, talking to my friends, journaling, reminding myself who I am, and a whole bunch of other things. The key is to do the work and not give up. For example, me feeling like no one could love me or like me, the feelings of abandonment that plague me—I still fight those feelings every day. I have to do the work of reminding myself I am loved and saying those affirmations about myself and telling myself I am worth loving. I'm still working on myself every day. I realize it's a process, but I'm definitely not where I was before. Every day is a journey in the right direction. I go to therapy, pray, read, journal, paint, and do other things that help in the healing process. Find what works for you. I read a lot of Joyce Meyer books which helped me see things differently and know I can actually be healed. Today I can honestly say I have three different families whom I love and great friends who help me grow every day. I am so thankful for everything I went through because it made me a stronger, independent, loving, and compassionate person. I wouldn't trade any of my lessons for anything because they made me who I am.

For all of the ladies and men out there struggling to know who you are and wondering if you're loved, you are! God did not forget about you. Hang on and fight because you are stronger than your circumstances. You can and will make it. Just believe in yourself. I made it and am still making it. It's a long hard road full of ups and downs and a lot of pain, but you can do it. *Don't give up!*

Also try and find people who will support your journey. If you don't have anyone, realize you are strong and that you made it this far. Keep going. Write down affirmations about yourself and repeat them every day until you believe them. Cry, scream, and do what you need to do to become free and live a whole healthy life.

About the Author

Tina is a young woman who has always had a love for people and a desire to see them free from everything that's holding them back from being who they truly are. Tina resides in Florida with her family and friends.

CPSIA information can be obtained
at www.ICGtesting.com
Printed in the USA
LVHW041113221121
704098LV00003B/233

9 781638 146933